mambo

mixers

Recipes for 50 Luscious Latin Cocktails and 20 Tantalizing Tapas

mambo
mixers

arlen Gargagliano   *Photographs by* Dasha Wright

Stewart, Tabori & Chang

NEW YORK

This book is dedicated to my loving and supportive husband, Seth Markusfeld,
and my children, Sofia and Wes, who fill my life with love, amazement, and delight.

Pictured on page 2 *(from left to right)*: Strawberry Daiquiri, Sangría Blanca, Mojito

Text copyright © 2005 Arlen Gargagliano
Editor: Jennifer Lang
Design: woolypear
Production: Jane Searle

Photographs copyright © 2005 Dasha Wright
Food Stylist: Brett Kurzweil
Prop Stylist: Lynda White
Photo Assistant: David DuToit

Published in 2005 by
Stewart, Tabori & Chang
115 West 18th Street
New York, NY 10011
www.abramsbooks.com

Canadian Distribution:
Canadian Manda Group
One Atlantic Avenue, Suite 105
Toronto, Ontario M6K 3E7
Canada

Library of Congress Cataloging-in-Publication Data
Gargagliano, Arlen.
    Mambo mixers : recipes for 50 luscious Latin cocktails and 20 tantalizing
    tapas /Arlen Gargagliano ; photographs by Dasha Wright.
        p. cm.
    Includes index.
    ISBN 1-58479-398-8
        1. Cocktails. 2. Appetizers. 3. Cookery, Spanish. I. Title.
TX951.G25 2005
641.8'74—dc22   2004021369

The text of this book was composed in Filosofia.

Printed in China
10 9 8 7 6 5 4 3 2 1
First Printing

Stewart, Tabori & Chang is a subsidiary of

LA MARTINIÈRE
G R O U P E

contents

Introduction

Lift your glass, close your eyes, and take a sip. Just one taste of a mint-infused mojito or a luscious lime-kissed caipirinha, and you're transported to the tropical destination of your dreams. Magical, elegant, sexy, and above all, *delicioso*, Latin cocktails are meant to be relished. From Mexico to Argentina, the Latin American philosophy of life is expressed in how drinks are designed, served, and enjoyed.

Hora de cócteles—cocktail hour—is a time to relax, celebrate life, and catch up with old or new friends. Take a step into a bar in Buenos Aires during the early evening and you'll hear the buzz of conversation sparked with laughter. You'll also see an assortment of empanadas—savory pastry pockets filled with a variety of ingredients— as well as homemade and perfectly salted thick potato chips and small dishes of olives on the bar and tables. Singles, couples, and small groups of people gather. Regardless of the weather outside, it's always embracingly sunny inside.

Though the scene may vary slightly throughout the Americas, the tradition remains the same: Cocktails are served with *algo para picar*, something to munch on. The drinks, like the foods that accompany them, are designed to complement rather than dominate the moment. The snacks should be attractive, tasty, and satisfying without being filling. Finally, the flavors of the tapas should marry well with sips of the sublime cocktails.

In the United States, we're just beginning to recognize the treasures of Latin American cocktails. Certainly margaritas and piña coladas can now be found in virtually every bar, while the mojito and caipirinha are not too far behind. Similarly, the custom of the *piqueo*, or the eating of a small amount, while drinking an alcoholic beverage and chatting with friends has become a ritual. Still, we've got so much more to explore; *Mambo Mixers* offers you the first steps to expanding your cocktail world!

It's hard not to be seduced by cultures that offer such welcoming celebrations of life. With an emphasis on get-togethers with friends and family, food becomes yet another expression of love. Even though they don't take hours to make, cocktails and appetizers are prepared with care for both taste and visual appeal.

I've been in love with everything Latino for as long as I can remember. My parents, both born and raised in New York City, embraced many aspects of Spanish-speaking cultures. Though I grew up in a home that primarily featured Italian cooking (my father is of Italian heritage, while my mother is from a Russian-Jewish background), my parents raised us to appreciate the rich diversity of the myriad cultures that surrounded us. But for me it was my high school Spanish teacher, Rosa Andrews, whose passion for life and literature guided me into what has become an inextricable part of my personality. Rosa not only facilitated my falling in love with a language, she also taught me how to look at life in a different way; she made me hungry to learn more. Thanks to her encouragement, I went on to live and study in Barcelona, Spain. After moving back to New York for a few years, to finish my undergraduate degree and teaching certification, I traveled to Peru—the home of Cynthia, my college roommate—for a week's vacation, and ended up spending a year teaching English in Lima. Since then I've been lucky enough to travel several times a year to different destinations in Mexico as well as Central and South America. Each time I try to bring a piece—in the form of recipes, books, stories, and experiences—home with me so that I can hold onto the smiles I felt so keenly during my visits.

In addition to traveling to many parts of Latin America, I've been learning about its culinary treasures right here in New York. I've been privileged to spend the past several years collaborating on the cookbooks of chef and restaurateur Rafael Palomino.

From tours through Little Colombia in Jackson Heights, Queens, to spending hours working on recipes in his New York restaurant kitchens, I have learned a great deal from Rafael about the subtlety and balance of Latin American cooking. Working with flavors and foods from both his native Colombia and the other Spanish-speaking countries that make up Central and South America, Rafael has been a constant inspiration as far as getting me to play with ingredients that are new to me. In fact I now can't imagine a time when cilantro, chipotle, yuca, and corn weren't staples in my own kitchen! Rafael also taught me that food should be as delightful to behold as it is to savor; this is another philosophy you will find in the creation of both cocktails and tapas in this book.

My years of being enamored with everything Latin are apparent in *Mambo Mixers*. Though this collection of fifty cocktails and twenty tapas (indicated by the ⭐) represents just a small sampling of what the Americas have to offer, it's a great way to start an exploration that will, I hope, be part of a lifelong adventure. These recipes are designed to be accessible to all, from the home cook to the experienced chef. The ingredients are neither overwhelmingly numerous nor difficult to find, and substitutions are suggested. All steps are clearly explained and include make-ahead tips so that hosts can join the party and not spend the whole time in the kitchen. After all, creating a party is like dancing: One step—or dish— smoothly blends into another. *Mambo Mixers* will give you ideas for the pairing of cocktails and tapas so that your cocktail party will flow.

Savor this sumptuous sojourn south of the border. Enjoy celebrating the cocktails and cultures of our Latin American neighbors. You may find yourself falling deeply in love with tastes you never knew before or discovering exciting twists on familiar flavors. Soon you'll become quite comfortable and confident with these recipes, and you'll start to experiment with your own variations and even new flavor combinations. The idea, after all, is to have fun.

Champagne is always festive! Light, simple, elegant, and tasty, champagne cocktails are easy to prepare for a party of two to twenty. This section gives you four wonderful champagne-and-juice combinations to choose from.

champagne drinks

Empanaditas de Carne (page 12) and Argentine-Style Bellini

Argentine-style Bellini

This Italian-born cocktail combination is very popular in Buenos Aires, Argentina. Though you can find many variations on this classic, some of which include peach schnapps and other liqueurs, the simplest one seems to be the most elegant and tasty. Served in a champagne flute, this light cocktail is a great way to start any evening—or party.

Serves 1

- 3 ounces peach nectar
- 5 ounces cold Spanish sparkling wine or dry champagne
- 1 thin peach slice and 1 raspberry, for garnish

Pour the peach nectar into an 8-ounce champagne glass or flute. Slowly add the sparkling wine or champagne. Stir, garnish with the peach slice and raspberry, and serve immediately.

empanaditas de carne

The empanada, next to the grilled steak, is a must at any Argentine party! Though the style and fillings vary depending on the region—and one's taste—empanadas, originally brought from Spain (via Arab cultures), have become one of Argentina's national dishes. This recipe for a stuffing of ground beef, olives, and raisins balances beautifully with the empanada crust. Ideal cocktail party fare, these empanaditas (small empanadas) can be frozen—simply enclose in an airtight container and defrost prior to baking. They're also easy to reheat in the oven or microwave. (If you prefer, you can buy premade empanada dough and cut it, using a 3-inch cookie cutter, for these small empanadas.)

See photo on page 10
Makes about 40 empanaditas

Dough

2 ¼ cups unbleached
      all-purpose flour
 ½ teaspoon kosher salt
2 teaspoons sugar
1 ½ sticks unsalted butter, chilled
      and cut into small pieces
    About ¼ cup ice water

Glaze

1 egg yolk
1 tablespoon water

Filling

2 tablespoons olive oil
1 sweet onion, chopped
½ pound lean ground beef
1 teaspoon sweet paprika
⅛ teaspoon cayenne pepper
½ teaspoon ground cumin
¼ cup dry white wine
2 hard-cooked eggs, coarsely chopped
½ cup pitted green, kalamata, or
      niçoise olives, or a combination
      of the three, chopped
½ cup raisins, chopped

Preheat the oven to 350°F. Prepare the dough: Combine the flour, salt, and sugar in a food processor. Add the butter and pulse just until the mixture resembles coarse meal. (You can also knead by hand.) Add the cold water one teaspoon at a time and continue pulsing until the dough forms a ball. Remove from the food processor, wrap with plastic wrap, and refrigerate for at least 1 hour or overnight.

Meanwhile, prepare the filling: Heat the olive oil over medium heat in a large frying pan. Add the onion and sauté until softened, about 5 minutes. Add the beef, paprika, pepper, and cumin and cook, stirring frequently, until the beef starts to brown. Add the white wine and cook until the wine is absorbed. Set aside and let cool to room temperature.

Prepare the dough for the filling: On a lightly floured surface, roll out the dough to a thickness between $1/16$ and $1/8$ inch. Use a martini glass or a 3-inch cookie cutter to cut the dough. Reroll the dough in order to use as much of it as you can. Place the rounds onto a parchment paper–covered baking sheet.

To assemble the empanadas, spoon about 1 heaping teaspoon of the beef, along with $1/2$ teaspoon of the eggs, $1/2$ teaspoon of the olives, and a few raisins in the center of the circle. Spread the mixture a bit, but leave a $1/2$-inch edge around. If the dough starts to crack, reseal it with a patch of dough or water. Seal by twisting the edge between your thumb and forefinger. (You can dip your fingertips in the egg glaze to help glue the edges as well.) Then press the edges with the tines of a fork. Repeat until all the empanadas are filled.

Prepare the egg glaze by mixing the egg yolk with the water. Place the empanadas on a lightly greased or parchment paper–coated baking sheet. Brush each empanada with the egg glaze, and bake for 15 to 20 minutes, or until golden. Serve hot.

mango champagne cocktail

This cocktail, made with a nice dry champagne, a couple of limes, and some mango nectar, is muy rico *(very delicious)! If you find ripe mangos, try making your own purée by simply peeling and coarsely chopping one, and liquefying it in the blender. You can serve this cocktail before or after dinner, with a variety of treats.*

Serves 1

- 4 ounces fresh mango purée or chilled mango nectar
   Juice of ½ lime
- 4 ounces cold Spanish sparkling wine or dry champagne
- 1 half-moon lime slice, for garnish

Pour the fruit purée or nectar into a chilled martini or wine glass. Add the lime juice. Top with the sparkling wine or champagne. Stir, garnish with the lime slice, and serve.

Pineapple Champagne Cocktail

Champagne cocktails, made with a variety of juices, can be found throughout Latin America. This cousin of the mimosa has just the right mixture of fizz and fruit flavors to whet appetites and get the party started.

Serves 1

- 2   ounces chilled pineapple juice
- 2   ounces fresh orange juice
- 4   ounces cold Spanish sparkling wine or dry champagne
- 1   half-moon orange slice, for garnish

Pour the fruit juices into a chilled martini or wine glass. Top with the champagne, stir, garnish with the orange slice, and serve.

passion fruit champagne cocktail

Whenever I visit Peru, one of my first stops is Lima's Mercado Central—the main market—in the downtown area. Aside from the joys of navigating the food-filled aisles, listening to the vendors' calls to buyers, and inhaling the mixed aromas of fresh ingredients, I love to plant myself in front of the fruit stalls—which could spark anyone's palate fantasies! This super-simple tropical mimosa is the result of one of those market visits. I bought fresh passion fruits and strained them into a glass before adding sparkling wine. Here in the States, if you can't find passion fruit nectar, you can probably find a tropical fruit blend. This cocktail is a great party treat with Empanaditas de Carne (page 12), Crisp Toasts with Chimichurri (page 18), and Panuchos (page 48).

Serves 1

4	ounces passion fruit nectar (or tropical fruit blend)
4	ounces cold Spanish sparkling wine or dry champagne
2 to 4	raspberries, for garnish

Pour the fruit nectar into an 8-ounce champagne flute. Top with the champagne, stir, garnish with the raspberries, and serve.

Crisp Toasts with Chimichurri (page 18) and Passion Fruit Champagne Cocktail

CRISP TOASTS WITH CHIMICHURRI

The blending of herbs in a classic chimichurri *is enchanting! Though this traditional Argentine pesto is often made with dried herbs, this interpretation uses mostly fresh ones. Simple to make, and versatile—use it as a dipping sauce for everything from chips to Yuca Fries (page 84), or as a marinade for steak or chicken.*

See photo on page 17
Makes about 1 ½ cups *chimichurri*

1 long French baguette, sliced into ¼-inch-thick rounds

3 garlic cloves, chopped
Leaves from 1 sprig oregano

2 bay leaves

2 teaspoons sweet paprika
Leaves from 6 sprigs thyme

15 basil leaves, plus extra, julienned, for garnish

1 bunch fresh parsley, coarsely chopped, plus extra for garnish

½ teaspoon cumin seeds
Kosher salt and freshly ground pepper to taste

½ cup white balsamic vinegar

¾ cup olive oil

Preheat the oven to 350°F. Spread the baguette rounds on a baking sheet. Toast for about 10 minutes on each side, or until lightly browned. Let cool and store in an airtight container until you're ready to use them.

Combine the remaining ingredients, except for the basil and parsley garnish, in a food processor or blender and process until smooth. Use the *chimichurri* immediately, or cover and refrigerate for up to 1 week. Return to room temperature, mix well, spread on arranged bread rounds, and garnish prior to serving.

There's got to be some kind of spark to make a cocktail into a classic! This list includes all-time favorites, as well as some interpretations that are quickly winning new fans.

classics & variations

Pisco Sour and Peruvian Skewered Beef (page 22)

pisco sour

Pisco sours are a must at any fiesta in Lima, Peru! My favorite bartender, José, shakes these up by hand in the Miraflores restaurant, La Gloria. However, when making several for a crowd, the blender is ideal. These ubiquitous Limeñan classics, now taking points north by storm, are light, tart, and quite powerful. I like to serve pisco sours in chilled martini glasses, with Peruvian Skewered Beef (page 22), Ceviche Limeño (page 24), or Yuca Fries with Peruvian Peppered Cheese Sauce (page 84), but they can be married with virtually any appetizer.

Serves 4

- 1 egg white
- 1 ½ tablespoons superfine sugar, or to taste (if the limes are very acidic, you will need more sugar)
- 1 cup pisco (Peruvian brandy), or to taste
  Juice of 3 limes
- 2 cups ice cubes
  Angostura bitters or nutmeg, for garnish

Chill four tumblers or martini glasses in the freezer for 10 minutes. In a blender, combine the egg white and sugar. Add the pisco, lime juice, and ice and mix well; the ice should be crushed and the top should be frothy. Pour into the chilled glasses, and top with a dash of bitters or a pinch of nutmeg. Serve immediately.

peruvian skewered beef

Anticuchos—grilled skewered beef—and Pisco Sours (page 21) are heavenly! The taste of the marinated meat, combined with the smoky flavors of the grill, is ideal for matching with a variety of cocktails. (Though traditionally prepared with beef hearts, this version seems much more popular in the United States.) For a great food combo, serve your anticuchos with Yuca Fries with Peruvian Peppered Cheese Sauce (page 84).

See photo on page 20
Serves 8 to 10

2   teaspoons *aji amarillo* (available in large supermarkets
      and Latin American markets)
1   teaspoon ground cumin
4   cloves garlic, crushed
1   cup red wine vinegar
1   tablespoon minced red or green bell pepper
    Kosher salt to taste
2   pounds ½-inch-thick boneless sirloin steak, trimmed of fat
      and cut into ½-inch cubes

In a large glass or ceramic bowl, combine the *ají*, cumin, garlic, vinegar, minced pepper, and salt. Mix well. Add the beef and toss with the marinade until the beef is well coated. Marinate in the refrigerator for at least 1 hour and up to 24 hours.

Remove the beef from the marinade and reserve the marinade. Thread the beef onto skewers (three or four to a skewer). Brush with the marinade and broil or grill, turning to cook on all sides for about 4 minutes, or until the desired doneness is reached. You could insert a rosemary sprig on the top of the skewers as garnish, or you might want to remove the meat from the skewers and serve on a platter, with toothpicks.

ceviche limeño

Cool, silky, and so tasty, ceviche—a marinated fish dish—is a wonderful cocktail-party treat. In most ceviches, the fish is "cooked" by the acid of the citrus juices. In Lima, where there are many cebicherías *(restaurants that serve ceviche), it is served along with a chunk of* camote *(sweet potato) and some* choclo *(corn). Serve this in martini glasses, next to a tray of Pisco Sours (page 21).*

Makes 8 to 10 servings

1   red onion, julienned
1   celery stalk, very finely diced
1   clove garlic, minced
1   teaspoon *ají amarillo* (sold
        in jars in Latin American
        markets), or to taste
1   red bell pepper,
        cut into very thin strips
1   green bell pepper,
        cut into very thin strips

Juice of 15 limes (about 1 ½ cups)
Kosher salt and freshly
        ground black pepper to taste
1   tablespoon very finely chopped fresh
        cilantro, plus another tablespoon
        coarsely chopped for garnish
2   pounds sashimi-grade
        Chilean sea bass, skinned
        and cut into ½-inch chunks

Combine half the onion, the celery, garlic, *ají*, the peppers, 1 cup of the lime juice, salt and pepper, and 1 tablespoon of the cilantro in a large glass bowl and mix well. Add the fish and make sure it's well-covered with the juice. Cover and refrigerate for between 30 minutes and 1 hour, stirring occasionally, until the fish starts to turn opaque on the outside. Taste and correct seasoning as needed. Spoon into martini glasses, top with remaining julienned onion and additional lime juice, sprinkle with cilantro, and serve.

peruvian screwdriver

The yugueño *—made of pisco (Peruvian brandy) and fresh orange juice—is as light and refreshing as its vodka-based cousin, the screwdriver. Try using blood oranges for a slightly different flavor (and gorgeous color). Great as a spring or summertime cocktail, it's best served straight-up in a chilled martini glass.*

Serves 1

- 2   ounces fresh-squeezed orange juice
- 1   ounce pisco
-     Ice cubes
- 1   half-moon orange slice, for garnish

Fill a shaker with orange juice, pisco, and ice cubes. Shake vigorously until well mixed. Strain into a well-chilled martini glass. Add the orange slice and serve immediately.

caipirinha

Pronounced ky-pee-REE-nya, *the name dances around your mouth as deliciously as the drink will. Hailed as the national cocktail of Brazil, the caipirinha can be sipped at sultry summertime parties or during the cold winter months; its tropical flavors transcend all seasons. Serve in cocktail or wine glasses.*

Serves 1

1	lime, cut into 8 wedges
2 ½	heaping teaspoons superfine sugar, or to taste
2	ounces *cachaça* (Brazilian rum) or light rum
	Ice cubes

Place the lime wedges and sugar in a tall bar glass. Use a pestle or the end of a wooden spoon to mash the lime and sugar together. Add the *cachaça* and stir. Add ice, cover, and shake. Pour into a glass and serve immediately.

pineapple caipirinha

Brazil is magical for so many reasons, but primarily for its people and their hospitality. When visiting homes in Brazil, you'll find that caipirinhas are made not only the traditional way, with limes, but also with a variety of tropical fruits depending on the hosts' preference, and of course, availability. You may want to serve these with a large straw—or even a spoon—so that your guests don't miss any of the cachaça-soaked fruit.

Serves 4

½ fresh pineapple, plus extra pieces for garnish, peeled, cored,
      and cut into cubes
1 cup *cachaça* (Brazilian rum)
1 cup crushed ice cubes
    Club soda
4 half-moon lime slices, for garnish

Divide the pineapple into four tumblers. Using a pestle or the end of a wooden spoon, mash the pineapple pieces until they're slightly muddled. Divide the *cachaça* and ice cubes among the glasses. Stir to mix, add a splash of club soda to each glass, garnish with the pineapple and a lime slice on the rim, and serve immediately.

KIWI CAIPIRINHA

During a visit to São Paulo, my dear friend, Elizabeth, introduced to me the kiwi caipirinha, which is a relatively recent version of the traditional lime classic. Clean-tasting and refreshing, this exotic cocktail is great anywhere and at any time of year. After you and your guests are done sipping, you may want to offer spoons so you can eat the remaining kiwi!

Serves 1

- 1 kiwi, peeled and quartered, plus 1 slice for garnish
- 1 teaspoon superfine sugar, or to taste
- 2 ounces *cachaça*
  Ice cubes

Place the kiwi and sugar in a tall bar glass. Use a pestle or the end of a wooden spoon to mash the kiwi and sugar together. Add the *cachaça* and stir. Add ice, cover, and shake. Pour into a glass, garnish with the kiwi slice, and serve immediately.

Kiwi Caipirinha and Brazilian Cheese Puffs (page 30)

Brazilian Cheese Puffs

My two children, Sofia and Wes, couldn't get enough of these when we visited Brazil. The best Brazilian cheese puffs—pão de queijo—are supposedly made in the state of Minas Gerais, but we found delicious ones along the coast in the state of São Paulo, thanks to our friend, Elizabeth, and her family. Warm and soft on the outside and cheesy in the center, these snacks are addictive. You can prepare them ahead of time, then bake them just prior to your guests' arrival. They're best served straight from the oven, with caipirinhas—or any fruit drink.

See photo on page 29
Makes about 6 dozen small cheese puffs

½	cup canola oil
⅓	cup water
⅓	cup milk
2	cups tapioca starch (available at Latin markets)
2	eggs, lightly beaten
2½	cups grated Sardo (Argentine Parmesan) or any Parmesan cheese

Preheat the oven to 375°F. In a medium saucepan, combine the oil, water, and milk and bring to a boil. Meanwhile, pour the starch into a large bowl. When the liquid has boiled, add it to the starch and mix well. Let it rest for about 15 minutes. Then stir in the eggs and the cheese.

Form into medium-size balls (about the circumference of a half dollar) and place them an inch apart on lightly greased or parchment paper-covered sheet pans. (At this point, you can cover and refrigerate them—even up to a day in advance— and then prepare them as your guests arrive.) Bake on the top rack of the oven until the tops start to brown, 15 to 20 minutes. Serve immediately. You can keep any remaining (if you have any left!) cheese puffs in an airtight container for up to 5 days. Reheat, wrapped in a paper towel, for about 15 seconds in the microwave.

classic cuban Daiquiri

As in the case of Cuban music, the flavors of the daiquiri will inspire you to get up and start dancing! Rumor has it that an engineer, who worked in a mine called Daiquirí in Cuba at the beginning of the twentieth century, invented this cocktail. Today this rum-and-lime juice cocktail has generations of variations. This version should be served straight up, in a chilled martini glass.

Serves 1

1 ½	ounces light rum
	Juice from 1 lime
1	teaspoon superfine sugar, or to taste
	Ice cubes
1	half-moon lime slice for garnish

Pour the rum, lime juice, and sugar into a shaker. Add ice, cover, and shake well. Strain into a chilled martini glass. Garnish with the lime slice and serve immediately.

Mango Daiquiri

Ripe mangos—or excellent-quality mango purée—make all the difference in this version of the daiquiri. The cocktail combines beautifully with Dominican Shrimp Croquettes (page 34).

Serves 1

- ½ cup mango purée or 1 ripe diced mango
- 2 ounces light rum
- 1 teaspoon fresh lime juice
- 1 teaspoon superfine sugar, or to taste
  Ice cubes (about 1 cup)
- 1 half-moon lime slice, for garnish

In a blender, combine all of the ingredients (except the lime slice) and process until smooth. Pour into a chilled wine glass, add the lime slice to the rim, and serve immediately with a straw.

Dominican Shrimp Croquettes

Spain was the place where I discovered croquettes—and was immediately taken with their flavor and texture (smooth and creamy on the inside and crunchy on the outside). A glass of Rioja, a few croquettes, and I was set. However, the world of croquettes stretches far from Europe and all up and down the Americas. The nice thing about these antojitos *(appetizers)—aside from the fact that they're delicious— is that they're quite adaptable. Once you get the recipe down, you can vary it depending on what's available (you can try them with other fish or vegetables, such as zucchini and mushrooms) and what you like. This version, adapted from a Dominican recipe, should be served with fresh wedges of lemon and lime and Mango-Cilantro Salsa (page 39).*

Makes about 35 croquettes

2 pounds Idaho potatoes, peeled and cut into 1-inch chunks

1 tablespoon sweet butter

2 egg yolks

1 cup grated mozzarella (or Muenster) cheese

2 tablespoons fresh chopped cilantro, plus additional cilantro for garnish

½ teaspoon kosher salt

Freshly ground black pepper to taste

4 tablespoons canola oil

1 small yellow onion, finely diced

½ pound medium shrimp, peeled, deveined and cut into ⅛- to ¼-inch pieces

¾ cup unbleached all-purpose flour

3 eggs, lightly beaten

1 cup bread crumbs

Lemon and lime wedges, for garnish

In a large pot of salted water, bring the potatoes to a boil. Cook for about 20 minutes, or until they're tender. Drain well and transfer the potatoes to a mixing bowl. Add the butter and mash with a potato masher or a fork. Add the egg yolks, cheese, cilantro, salt, and pepper, and stir well. Set aside.

Heat 1 tablespoon of oil in a frying pan over medium heat. Add the onion and cook, stirring frequently, until it starts to brown. Stir in the shrimp and cook until they turn pink, 3 to 5 minutes. Set aside.

Scoop up a golf ball-size portion of mashed potatoes (you can use a spoon, but your hands will work much better). Use your index finger to make a well in which you can stuff about a tablespoon of the shrimp mixture. Cover the hole with more potato. Repeat with the remaining potato and shrimp mixture and set aside.

Set up three shallow containers. Fill one with the flour, the other with the beaten eggs, and the last with bread crumbs. Roll the croquette first in the flour, followed by the egg, and finally the bread crumbs, until it's evenly coated. Continue until all the croquettes are dredged. Place them on a sheet pan or plate, cover them with a tent of plastic wrap, and put them in the fridge for 30 to 60 minutes.

Preheat the oven to 250°F. Heat 3 tablespoons of oil in a heavy skillet. Sauté the croquettes, a few at a time, for about 2 minutes on each side, or until golden-brown. Drain on paper towels and keep warm in the oven until finished. Sprinkle with cilantro, and serve with fresh lemon and lime wedges.

Strawberry Daiquiri

STRAWBERRY DAIQUIRI

This version of the daiquiri is as colorful as it is delicious. To keep it festive for those who don't drink alcohol, including the under-twenty-one (but over Shirley Temples) crowd, you can make a nonalcoholic version. Simply substitute about an ounce of water (you don't want it too watery) for the rum and Triple Sec, and the result is a superb strawberry drink!

Serves 1

- 2 ounces light rum
  Juice of 1 lime, plus 1 full-moon lime slice, for garnish
- 6 strawberries, stemmed and sliced, plus 1 for garnish
- 1 teaspoon superfine sugar, or to taste
- ½ ounce Triple Sec
- ½ cup ice cubes

Combine all of the ingredients (except the lime slice and 1 strawberry) in a blender and process until smooth. Pour into a chilled wine glass, garnish with the lime slice and the remaining strawberry, and serve immediately.

cilantro-potato pancakes

Tasty and versatile, these Mexican-style potato pancakes go well with
Mango-Cilantro Salsa (page 39) and just about any cocktail.

Makes about 20 small pancakes

1 ½ pounds Idaho potatoes,
        peeled and quartered
½ cup grated Monterey Jack cheese
½ cup grated Cheddar cheese
1 jalapeño pepper, seeded and
        diced, or ½ teaspoon
        chipotle purée (see page 70)
1 egg, beaten

1 bunch cilantro, stemmed and
        chopped, plus additional
        cilantro for garnish
1 teaspoon all-purpose flour
        (for shaping the potato cakes)
¼ cup canola oil
        Kosher salt to taste

In a medium saucepan filled with cold water, bring the potatoes to a boil. Cook for about 30 minutes, or until tender. Drain the potatoes, return them to the pan, and coarsely mash using a masher. The potatoes do not have to be smooth. Transfer the mashed potatoes to a bowl and add the grated cheese and the jalapeños. Add the egg and cilantro, and mix to form a dough.

When cool enough to handle, transfer the dough to a board. Divide the dough into twenty equal pieces. Using floured hands, shape into balls, and then flatten them into small cakes.

Heat 3 tablespoons of oil in a medium-size frying pan. Fry the potato cakes in batches, adding oil as needed, for about 2 minutes on each side, or until lightly browned. Place them on a platter, sprinkle with salt and cilantro, and serve immediately.

mango-cilantro salsa

Though this salsa goes beautifully with Dominican Shrimp Croquettes
(page 34) and Cilantro-Potato Pancakes (page 38), it's also wonderful on its
own, with tortilla chips.

Makes about 2 cups

- 1 ripe mango, peeled and diced
- 1 cucumber, seeded and diced
- ½ cup finely diced red onion
  Juice of 1 lime
  Juice of 1 orange
- 1 jalapeño pepper, seeded and diced (optional)
- 2 tablespoons olive oil
- 1 tablespoon white balsamic vinegar
  Kosher salt and freshly ground black pepper to taste
- ¼ cup fresh chopped cilantro leaves

In a medium-size mixing bowl, combine all of the ingredients (except the cilantro),
and let sit for about 15 minutes. Serve immediately, or cover and refrigerate for
up to 3 days. Bring to room temperature and stir in the cilantro just before serving.

Piña Colada

The Puerto Rican–born piña colada was for many years the quintessential tropical drink. This variation offers you the option of including fresh pineapple and coconut, for even more texture and taste. For a delicious nonalcoholic version, simply substitute extra pineapple juice for the rum. Though these can be very rich, they're certainly tasty!

Serves 1

- 2 ounces light or golden rum
- 4 ounces unsweetened pineapple juice
- 2 ounces cream of coconut
- ½ cup fresh pineapple chunks (optional)
- 1 teaspoon shredded sweetened coconut (optional)
- ½ cup ice cubes
- 1 pineapple slice, for garnish

Combine all of the ingredients (except the pineapple slice) in a blender. Process until smooth. Pour into a chilled wine glass, garnish with the pineapple slice, and serve.

Mango Colada (page 42) and Piña Colada

Mango Colada

The delectable flesh of the mango has been delighting people for thousands of years. It's not surprising that centuries ago, in Southeast Asia, kings and nobles began a custom of sending the choicest mangoes as gifts to privileged recipients. Even today the mango tree is considered sacred in India and remains a symbol of love and good fortune. Fans of this fabulous fruit will appreciate this colorful variation on the piña colada. Depending on your taste, include the extra fresh pineapple. You can make it in larger quantities (simply double the recipe) and keep it in the freezer for a bit before serving.

See photo on page 41
Serves 1

2   ounces light or golden rum
4   ounces mango nectar
2   ounces cream of coconut
½   cup fresh mango chunks, plus 1 additional slice for garnish (optional)
¼   cup diced pineapple
1   cup ice cubes

Combine all of the ingredients (except the mango slice) in a blender. Process until smooth. Pour into a chilled wine glass, garnish with the mango slice, and serve.

cuba libre

This extremely simple cocktail is not only wonderfully tasty and invigorating but is also easy to combine with virtually any appetizer.

Serves 1

½ lime, halved again, plus 1 half-moon lime slice, for garnish
2 ounces light rum
Cola to fill the glass

Squeeze the lime quarters into a glass filled with ice, and drop in the lime hulls. Pour the rum on top, and fill the glass with cola, stirring gently. Garnish with the lime slice and serve immediately.

Classic Margarita

Standing tall, a salt-rimmed martini glass looks regal and inviting when it's filled with a margarita. The Mexican margarita, which varies from city to city, and even from bar to bar, has three fundamental ingredients: tequila, Cointreau or Triple Sec (or another orange liqueur), and lime juice. The trick to making an excellent margarita is good tequila and fresh lime juice. Though the Mexican lime is somewhat sweeter than what we typically find here in the States, key limes, now more readily available, offer a slightly sweeter alternative to the usual find.

See photo on page 46
Serves 1

Juice of 1 lime, plus 2 lime wedges
1   teaspoon kosher salt (for glass rim)
1 ½   ounces tequila
½   ounce Cointreau or Triple Sec
1   cup ice cubes

Rub the rim of a chilled martini or margarita glass with a wedge of lime. Pour the salt onto a plate, and press the rim of the glass into it, turning gently until the rim is evenly coated. Shake off excess. In a cocktail shaker, combine the tequila, Triple Sec, lime juice, and ice cubes. Shake well. Strain into the prepared glass. Garnish with the remaining lime wedge and serve.

Passion Fruit Margarita

What could possibly go wrong when you put passion fruit and tequila together? Smooth and sexy, this cocktail—especially when served with the right company— is magical.

Serves 1

> Juice of ½ lime, plus 2 lime wedges
>
> 1 teaspoon kosher salt (for glass rim; optional)
>
> ½ cup passion fruit (or tropical fruit blend) nectar
>
> 1½ ounces tequila
>
> ¼ ounce Grand Marnier
>
> 1 cup ice cubes

Rub the rim of a chilled martini glass with a wedge of lime. Pour the salt onto a plate, and press the rim of the glass into it, turning gently until the rim is evenly coated. Shake off excess. In a cocktail shaker, combine the passion fruit, lime juice, tequila, Grand Marnier, and ice cubes. Shake well. Strain into the prepared glass. Garnish with the remaining lime wedge and serve.

clockwise from top: Watermelon Margarita, Classic Margarita (page 44), and Panuchos (page 48)

watermelon margarita

The Mexican artist Frida Kahlo once said, "Fruits are like flowers: they speak a provocative language and teach us things that are hidden." The watermelon—fresh, pink, and dotted with small black seeds—played a starring role in several of her paintings and is loved throughout Mexico as well as in many other Latin American countries. This gorgeous margarita is a great complement to any treat you serve with it.

Serves 2

4	tablespoons fresh lime juice,
	1 lime wedge, and 2 full-moon lime slices for garnish
2	teaspoons kosher salt (for glass rim)
3	ounces tequila
1 ½	cups diced, seeded watermelon
1 ½	tablespoons Cointreau
2 ½	teaspoons superfine sugar, or to taste
1	cup ice cubes

Rub the rims of two chilled margarita or cocktail glasses with a wedge of lime. Pour the salt onto a plate, and press the rims of the glasses into it, turning gently until the rims are evenly coated. Shake off excess. Combine the remaining ingredients (except the lime slices) in a blender. Process until smooth. Pour into the prepared glasses, garnish with the lime slices, and serve.

panuchos

Panuchos are small bites of chicken topped with orange juice and brown sugar-sweetened red onions. Though panuchos *are a typical* antojito, *appetizer, of the Yucatán region of Mexico, variations can be found in other parts of Mexico. Easy to prepare and very, very tasty,* panuchos *go well with any cocktail. They're also a great way to use leftover chicken! While they're normally served on homemade fried tortillas, I serve them on Arepas (page 106). Of course you can also spoon the chicken mixture onto large tortilla chips; though it's a bit messier, the result is just as* delicioso!

See photo on page 46
Makes 12 to 15 *panuchos*

For the onions

- 2 tablespoons vegetable oil
- 2 red onions, thinly sliced into rounds
- 2 oranges
- 1 teaspoon apple cider vinegar
- 1 teaspoon dark brown sugar

2 cups cooked shredded (into bite-size pieces) chicken breast

1 teaspoon achiote (ground annatto seeds; available at Latin American markets)

1 dozen Arepas (page 106), warm or at room temperature

½ cup refried black beans (page 53)

1 tablespoon chopped fresh cilantro

Pour the vegetable oil into a frying pan over medium heat. Sauté the onion, stirring constantly, for about 5 minutes, or until it starts to soften. Cut 1 orange in half and squeeze the juice over the onion. Add the vinegar and brown sugar. Let simmer until the liquid evaporates. Set aside.

In a medium-size bowl, combine the shredded chicken breast, achiote, and juice from the remaining orange and mix well. Arrange the *arepas* on a serving platter. Using a teaspoon, spread a spoonful of refried beans on each *arepa*. Then add a small amount of shredded chicken. Top with the onion, and a sprinkle of cilantro, and serve immediately.

MOJITO

The mojito (pronounced moh-HEE-toh*) was destined to take the United States by storm. After all, how could a country already enamored with the mint julep not fall for this Cuban classic? Just one sip of a mojito, which perfectly combines the flavors of rum, mint, and sugar, will prove why its popularity continues to explode. This aromatic drink should be served in a tall thin glass, with an extra mint sprig for garnish.*

Serves 1

4	fresh mint sprigs, plus extra for garnish
2	teaspoons superfine sugar
1	ounce fresh lime juice, plus additional lime wedges, for garnish
1 ½	ounces light rum
	Ice cubes
	Splash club soda

Remove the mint leaves from their stems, and place them in a tall bar glass. Add the sugar. Use a pestle or the end of a wooden spoon to lightly mash the mint leaves and sugar together. Add the lime juice, rum, and a cup of ice. Cover and shake. Top with club soda. Garnish with a mint sprig and lime wedges and serve immediately.

Mojito

pineapple mojito

This pineapple version of the Cuban classic is maravilloso! *The mint and the pineapple make a wonderful marriage of flavors. This cocktail can be served with the Costa Rican Refried Black Beans (page 53).*

Serves 1

4   fresh mint sprigs, plus extra for garnish
2   teaspoons superfine sugar, or to taste
    Juice of 1 lime
2   ounces pineapple juice
1 ½ ounces light rum
    Ice cubes
    Splash club soda
1   half-moon lime slice, for garnish

Remove the mint leaves from their stems, and place them in a shaker. Add the sugar. Use a pestle or the end of a wooden spoon to lightly mash the mint leaves and sugar together. Add the lime juice, pineapple juice, rum, and a cup of ice. Cover and shake well. Pour into a tall glass. Top with club soda. Garnish with a mint sprig and the lime slice and serve immediately.

costa rican refried black beans

*The graciousness of the Ticos (Costa Ricans) is both endearing and contagious!
You can't walk into a Costa Rican home without having some kind of treat offered to
you almost immediately. This recipe, inspired by our friends the Gutiérrez-Vargas
family, is one that you can whip up ahead of time, or when guests surprise you. Serve
with your favorite tortilla chips.*

Makes about 2 cups

- 2 tablespoons canola oil
- ¼ cup chopped red onion
- ¼ cup chopped red bell pepper
- 2 cloves garlic, minced
- 2 jalapeño chilies, seeded and minced
- ½ teaspoon kosher salt, or to taste
- 1 teaspoon chipotle purée
- 2 15.5-ounce cans black beans, undrained and puréed
- ¼ cup chopped fresh cilantro
- ¼ cup crumbled *queso fresco* (Mexican cheese, available in large supermarkets and Latin American markets) or grated mozzarella cheese

Heat the oil in a medium frying pan. Sauté the onion, pepper, garlic, chilies,
and salt for about 5 minutes, or until the onion has softened. Stir in the chipotle
purée and the beans and mix well. Cook over a low flame, stirring occasionally,
for about 15 minutes. Let cool slightly and transfer to a serving bowl. Top with
cilantro and *queso fresco* just before serving.

Machu Picchu

MACHU PICCHU

Reminiscent of a tequila sunrise, this Peruvian-born cocktail—named after one of the most exquisite places on earth—is quite festive! It's deep green (thanks to a bit of crème de menthe) on the top and orange in the middle, and the grenadine sits on the bottom (but soon starts to rise). This is a fun cocktail to make and serve with colorful straws and umbrellas.

Serves 1

Ice cubes

2 ounces pisco

4 ounces fresh-squeezed orange juice

1/4 ounce grenadine

1/4 ounce crème de menthe

Fill a tall glass with ice cubes. Pour in 1 ounce of the pisco, the orange juice, and the grenadine. In a cocktail shaker, combine the remaining pisco, crème de menthe, and three ice cubes and shake well (this will lighten the crème de menthe so that it floats on the top). Pour on top of the orange juice mixture in the tall glass, and add a straw, but don't stir or the colors will blend together.

tequila sunrise

Mexico is vibrant. One walk through the market or down a street—whether it's in the capital or in a smaller city or town—and you'll find that colors, like music, reach out and delight you. The tequila sunrise, with its changing golden tones, is a lot like its birthplace: bright, festive, and tasty. In making a tequila sunrise, or any tequila cocktail, use good-quality tequila. While blanco or reposado offer a gentle flavor, the añejos may be too woody for mixing.

Serves 1

    Ice cubes

2 ounces tequila

½ ounce fresh lime juice

5 ounces fresh orange juice

½ ounce grenadine

1 half-moon orange slice, for garnish

Fill a highball glass with ice cubes. Add the tequila, lime juice, and orange juice and stir. Float the grenadine on top (it will sink to the bottom, and then rise up, creating a sunrise effect) and garnish with the orange slice.

In both presentation and punch, these cocktails are Latin-style martinis. Serve them with several different appetizers and you'll keep your guests smiling (and, perhaps, dancing)!

martini-like cocktails

PISCO Martini

Elegant, slightly sweet, and powerful, this Peruvian martini complements any piqueo, *or assortment of appetizers.*

Serves 1

Ice cubes
2 ounces pisco
1 ounce red vermouth
6 drops Angostura bitters, or to taste
1 strip orange or lemon rind, for garnish

In a shaker filled with ice cubes, combine the pisco, vermouth, and bitters. Shake well to chill, and strain into a chilled martini glass. Garnish with the orange or lemon rind and serve immediately.

Pisco Martini and Scallop Tiradito (page 60)

scallop tiradito

This recipe hails from Mexico's west coast (Ixtapa), but I had the pleasure of enjoying it in the northern city of Monterrey. It's simple, clean, very elegant, and goes well with a Pisco Martini (page 58), Argentine-Style Bellini (page 11), or Mango Champagne Cocktail (page 14). Make sure the scallops are sashimi-grade quality. It will be easier to slice the scallops—with a very sharp knife—if they're semi-frozen (and then thawed completely prior to serving). You can serve this dish by passing it around on a platter (with cocktail forks) or dishing it out onto individual plates.

See photo on page 59
Serves 6 (2 scallops per person)

12	sashimi-grade sea scallops, cut thinly or into thirds
1	medium-size red onion, very thinly sliced
1	mango, peeled, and cut into 2-inch-long thin strips
	Kosher salt
	Extra-virgin olive oil
	Juice of 1 lime
	Hot sauce (Cholula or Tabasco; optional)
¼	cup chopped fresh cilantro leaves
12	large tortilla chips (preferably homemade)

Chill six small plates in the refrigerator for about an hour before serving. Place two sliced scallops on each plate. Decorate with red onion and slices of mango. Add a pinch of salt to each plate. Drizzle with olive oil, lime juice, and a couple of drops of hot sauce. Sprinkle with cilantro. Decorate with two tortilla chips per plate. Serve immediately.

SOL Y SOMBRA

This cocktail tastes light and bubbly, but it does pack a punch! The traditional version of this martini-like Peruvian cocktail contains an intense red liqueur called guinda, *made from a kind of cherry. Though this interpretation creates a cocktail somewhat paler in color and slightly different in flavor than the original, it's winning over a whole new crowd of Sol y Sombra fans! Served with platters of Empanaditas de Carne (page 12) or Yuca Fries with Peruvian Peppered Cheese Sauce (page 84), this drink is sublime.*

Serves 1

	Ice cubes
2	ounces pisco
	Juice of 1 lemon, plus one ½-inch strip lemon rind for garnish
2 to 3	ounces ginger ale

In a shaker filled with ice cubes, combine the pisco and lemon juice. Shake briskly and strain into a chilled martini glass. Top with the ginger ale, garnish with the lemon rind, and serve.

Passion Fruit Cocktail

passion fruit cocktail

Passion fruit (maracuyá) *is as seductive as its name promises. Fresh* maracuyá *would be perfect for this drink, but a good-quality nectar—which is becoming easier and easier to find—also works very well.*

Serves 1

      Ice cubes
1 ½ ounces pisco
   3 ounces passion fruit (or tropical fruit blend) nectar
   1 full-moon lime slice, for garnish

In a shaker filled with ice cubes, combine the pisco and fruit nectar. Shake well and strain into a chilled martini glass. Place the lime slice in the cocktail. Serve immediately.

colombian aguardiente sour

Colombia's national liquor is aguardiente, *a sweet, powerful, anise-flavored brandy that tastes similar to the Greek liquor ouzo. Try some and you'll soon discover why Colombians sneak their favorite alcohol into everything from cocktails to desserts!*

Serves 2

4	ounces Colombian *aguardiente*
1 ½	ounces fresh lemon juice
1 ½	ounces fresh orange juice
1	egg white
2	tablespoons superfine sugar, or to taste
1	cup ice cubes
2	half-moon orange slices, for garnish

In a cocktail shaker, combine all of the ingredients except the orange slices. Shake well. Strain into two chilled martini glasses, garnish, and serve.

¡Prepárense! *Prepare yourselves! This selection promises to delight you and your guests. From the mango-rich rum cocktail to the Mexican beer cooler, you've got a selection here that will match any mood and taste.*

mixed drinks & coolers

Mango-Rum Cocktail

Stimulating, summery, and very smooth, this cocktail will transport you to the Caribbean in a heartbeat!

Serves 2

    Ice cubes

3 ounces light rum

½ teaspoon superfine sugar, or to taste

¾ cup mango nectar (or 1 cup puréed mango)

¼ ounce Cointreau

    Juice of ½ lemon, plus 2 half-moon lemon slices, for garnish

2 splashes club soda

In an ice-filled shaker, combine the rum, sugar, mango nectar, Cointreau, and lemon juice. Pour into two short glasses, garnish with the lemon slices, and top with club soda. Serve immediately.

GIN FIZZ

I used to think that there was nothing like a cool gin and tonic on a summer's evening, but then I discovered the gin fizz. This simple, thirst-quenching, and light coctél has cousins found throughout the Americas. Squeeze plenty of lemons and limes before your guests arrive to make the preparation even smoother.

Serves 1

Ice cubes
1   tablespoon fresh lime juice
1   tablespoon fresh lemon juice
1   teaspoon superfine sugar, or to taste
2   ounces gin
    Splash club soda
1   lime or lemon wedge, for garnish

In a shaker filled with ice, combine the citrus juices, sugar, and gin. Shake well and strain into a chilled glass filled with ice. Top with club soda, garnish with the lime or lemon wedge, and serve.

sangrita

Though I've been lucky enough to visit Mexico on several occasions over the years, it was only recently that I was introduced to the wonders of sangrita. *Literally translated as "little blood,"* sangrita *is a kind of spicy tomato juice (reminiscent of what you might use to make a Bloody Mary) which beautifully balances tequila. (Actually, I love the flavor so much that I'm happy to drink it on its own!)* Sangrita *is a key component in the* banderita, *or "little flag," which is made up of three shots: Fresh lime juice (almost green), tequila (white), and* sangrita *(red) are the three "stripes" of the Mexican flag that make up this combo. Though there are variations according to taste, I was taught to take a sip of the* sangrita, *then the lime juice, then the tequila, swish it around and swallow.* Sangrita *recipes vary in flavor and temperature from restaurant to restaurant; this combination is one of my favorites.*

Makes about 4 cups, or sixteen 2-ounce servings

- 2   cups tomato juice
- 1   small onion, finely chopped
- 1   jalapeño, seeded and finely chopped, or 3 dashes Tabasco sauce, or to taste
- 1   teaspoon Worcestershire sauce
- 1   cup fresh-squeezed orange juice
    Juice of 3 limes
    Kosher salt and freshly ground black pepper to taste

Combine all of the ingredients in a blender and process to blend. Pour into a pitcher, cover, and refrigerate for at least 1 hour or up to 5 days.

Banderita: A shot of Sangrita, tequila, and fresh lime juice, with Pepitas (page 70)

pepitas

Pepitas—*pumpkin seeds*—*are a popular ingredient in many Mexican dishes.
This easy-to-prepare version of toasted* pepitas *is great to serve in small decorative
bowls while guests are enjoying their cocktails. This recipe includes the smoky
spark of* chipotles en adobo: *smoked red jalapeño peppers, prepared in a spiced
vinegar, tomato, and ancho chile sauce and sold in 7-ounce cans in large
supermarkets or Latin American groceries.*

See photo on page 69
Serves 4

- 1   cup pumpkin seeds
- 3   garlic cloves, crushed
- 1   *chipotle en adobo*, finely diced (you can also purée a can of chipotles
      and use about ½ teaspoon of the purée)
- ¼   teaspoon kosher salt, or to taste
- 1   teaspoon turbinado sugar
- 1   lime wedge

Heat a medium-size heavy frying pan, and pour in the pumpkin seeds. Let toast
for about 5 minutes, stirring constantly. Stir in the garlic and cook for another
2 minutes. Add the *chipotle*, salt, and sugar and mix well so that all the seeds are
coated. Remove from the heat and pour into a bowl. Serve immediately, or let cool
and store in an airtight container for up to 1 week. Before serving, squeeze the
wedge of lime on top.

vampiro

You may want to serve this sparky tomato-juice cocktail at your next brunch,
along with Tortilla Española (page 72). Found in bars and restaurants throughout
Mexico, this popular drink is so named because it's made with sangrita, *which*
means "little blood." Some like their vampiros *super spicy, while others vary*
the citrus juice added. This recipe is for one; simply multiply it depending on the
number of guests you have, and serve it from a pitcher into ice-filled and
garnished glasses.

Serves 1

½ lemon, plus one ½-inch strip rind for garnish
   Ice cubes
4 ounces *Sangrita* (page 68)
2 ounces tequila
   Splash fresh grapefruit juice

Squeeze the lemon into a glass filled with ice cubes. Add the *sangrita*
and tequila. Top with the grapefruit juice. Stir, garnish with the lemon rind,
and serve immediately.

tortilla española

You'd be hard pressed to find a tapas bar in Spain that didn't serve tortilla española. *This Spanish classic has made its way into bars and homes throughout Latin America. Though the ingredients are minimal, there is one thing that you must learn to do in order to make it successfully: flip it without letting it slide onto your stovetop. This is easily mastered after a couple of tries. Served either heated or at room temperature, this appetizer is ideal because you make it ahead of time and then let it sit. Served sandwich-style between slices of bread, by itself in small wedges, or along with a dipping salsa, this is sure to be a hit at any cocktail party— or brunch.*

Serves 8 to 10

- ½ cup olive oil
- 4 medium potatoes, peeled and cut into ⅛-inch-thick slices
- 1 large onion, thinly sliced
  Kosher salt to taste
- 5 large eggs

In a medium-size skillet, about 10-inches wide with sloping sides, heat ¼ cup of the oil. Add the potato slices one at a time, making a single layer on the bottom of the pan. Add salt, then add the onion slices on top, followed by the remaining potato slices. Add additional salt, if desired. Cook over medium heat, turning occasionally, until the potatoes are tender and lightly golden. Remove the potatoes and onions with a spatula, and let drain on paper towels.

In a large bowl, beat the eggs with a fork until foamy. Add the potato-onion mixture to the egg in the bowl, pressing down so that it's covered by the egg. Let sit for about 10 to 15 minutes.

Heat 3 tablespoons of the oil in the pan; it must be very hot or the eggs will stick. Add the egg-and-potato mixture. Use a spatula to spread it out evenly. Lower the heat and shake the pan frequently to prevent sticking.

After about 8 minutes, or when the eggs start to brown underneath and they're mostly set on top, invert a plate of the same size or slightly larger than the skillet on top and flip the tortilla onto the plate. Add about a tablespoon more of oil to the pan, and slide the tortilla back into it for about 5 minutes to brown on the other side.

Turn the tortilla over several more times to cook it briefly on each side; this helps to shape it as well as cook it more. It should be lightly golden on the outside yet still juicy on the inside. Transfer to a serving plate and let cool slightly. Cut into thin wedges or squares to be served using toothpicks.

Bloody María

BLOODY María

Like its vodka-enhanced cousin, this Mexican cocktail can be varied according to your or your guests' preferences.

Serves 1

	Ice cubes
2	ounces tequila
4	ounces tomato juice
	Juice of ½ lemon
	Juice of ½ lime
1 to 2	dashes Tabasco
	Kosher salt to taste
1	celery stalk or half-moon lime slice for garnish

Combine all of the ingredients (except the celery stalk or lime slice) in a shaker. Pour into a tall glass, garnish with the celery stalk or lime slice, and serve.

salsa criolla

Along with chimichurri, *Argentina boasts another salsa that is served at its famous parties:* salsa criolla. *This salsa, easy to prepare and tasty, can be served by itself on chips or with grilled meats, empanadas, or even with Tortilla Española (page 72). And just as Argentine chefs and home cooks do, you can vary the ingredients according to your taste.*

Makes about 3 cups

- ½ cup finely diced red onion
- ½ cup finely diced white onion
- 1 small green bell pepper, finely diced (about ½ cup)
- 1 red bell pepper, finely diced (about 1 cup)
- 1 garlic clove, minced
- 1 tablespoon finely chopped fresh parsley
- ½ teaspoon chopped fresh oregano leaves
- 1 tomato, diced
- ½ cup olive oil
- ¼ cup red wine vinegar
  Kosher salt and freshly ground black pepper to taste

Combine all of the ingredients in a medium-size mixing bowl and stir. Cover and refrigerate for at least 2 hours. Bring to room temperature before serving.

PISCO, MINT & STRAWBERRY COCKTAIL

The pisco marries nicely with the flavors of the mint, strawberry, and lime juice in this fantastic frozen drink. Try this cocktail when strawberries and mint are at their peak—you may want to add more of both!

Serves 1

1 ½	ounces pisco
	Juice of 1 lime
4 to 6	strawberries, plus an additional one for garnish
1 ½	teaspoons superfine sugar, or to taste
1	cup ice cubes
4	mint leaves, finely chopped

Combine the pisco, lime juice, strawberries (except the one for garnish), sugar, and ice in a blender and process until smooth. Pour into a chilled wine glass, stir in the mint leaves, and garnish by placing the strawberry on the rim. Serve with a straw.

COLOMBIAN RUM & GRAPEFRUIT COCKTAIL

Light and not too sweet, this cocktail is terrific at a brunch with Sopa Paraguaya (page 80), Brazilian Cheese Puffs (page 30), and Walnut- & Cabrales-Coated Grapes (page 96).

Serves 1

	Ice cubes
1 ½	ounces light rum
3	ounces fresh grapefruit juice
1	teaspoon superfine sugar, or to taste
¼	grapefruit slice, for garnish

In a tall glass filled with ice, combine the rum, grapefruit juice, and sugar. Stir well, garnish with the grapefruit slice, and serve immediately.

papaya & orange caribbean cooler

With flesh that's butter-smooth and a taste that resembles a cross between a melon and a peach, the luscious papaya combines beautifully with many other foods—and liquids! The papaya boasts not only fabulous flavor but also a host of curative properties. Its medicinal virtues include several types of antioxidants. Indians of Latin America have long revered the papaya; Aztecs used the fruit to cure a wide range of ailments, ranging from digestion problems to skin irritations. Perfectly blended with the flavors of fresh citrus juices, this cocktail is tasty with or without the rum.

Serves 2

1	ripe medium-size papaya, peeled, seeded, and diced
1	cup freshly squeezed orange juice
3	ounces light or golden rum
	Juice of 1 lime
1	tablespoon superfine sugar, or to taste
1½ to 2	cups ice cubes
2	half-moon orange slices, for garnish

Combine all of the ingredients in a blender (except the orange slices) and process until smooth. Garnish with the orange slices and serve with straws.

sopa paraguaya

*Don't be fooled by the name of this dish; it's not a soup! Versions of cornbread
can be found throughout Latin America. This interpretation of* sopa paraguaya,
*which can be made with instant cornmeal or polenta, is easy and very tasty.
It's also adaptable! Once you've made it a couple of times, you can vary the amounts
(and types) of cheese and even vegetables that you include. This style of cornbread
is more like quiche than bread; it's moist and rich enough to be served by itself.
You simply need to let it cool just a bit (but not too much; it should be served hot from
the oven), cut it into squares, and place it on a serving platter. Leftovers can be
stored in the refrigerator and heated up in the oven or microwave.*

Makes about 12 small servings

2	tablespoons olive oil
1	onion, finely chopped
1	red bell pepper, finely chopped
1½	teaspoons baking powder
6	tablespoons instant cornmeal or instant polenta
1¾	cups milk
2	tablespoons unsalted butter, plus more for greasing
1	teaspoon chili powder
½	teaspoon paprika
1	teaspoon sugar
	Kosher salt to taste

½ cup shredded Monterey Jack cheese

½ cup shredded Cheddar cheese

1 ½ cups fresh or frozen corn kernels

3 eggs, beaten

Preheat the oven to 375°F. Grease a shallow 2-quart baking dish. Heat the olive oil in a medium-size sauté pan over medium heat. Add the onion and pepper and sauté for about 10 minutes, or until soft. Set aside.

In a bowl, sift together the baking powder and cornmeal.

Pour the milk into a large saucepan over medium heat. Add the butter, chili powder, paprika, sugar, and salt. Bring just to a boil. Remove from the heat and slowly pour in the cornmeal, stirring constantly. Add the sautéed onion and pepper, and cheeses. Stir in the corn and eggs and mix well. Pour into the greased baking dish. Bake for 30 minutes, or until set and lightly browned. Let cool slightly before cutting into squares and serving.

Mexican Beer Cooler

On those summer days when you walk outside and the heat and humidity blanket you, and you can feel a steady trickle of sweat roll off your forehead and behind your knees, micheladas are ideal! I had my first michelada, a Mexican-style beer cooler, two years ago—thanks to Alex in Mexico City—after making a presentation to close to a thousand English teachers. Since then I've been devoted to this wonderful thirst-quenching mixture and have served it to the delight of many on steamy New York summer evenings. If you are in eastern Mexico, a michelada is beer combined with a sangrita-like mixture; there you may want to order a chelada, which is the lime juice, ice, and beer combination described here. Some salt the rim of the glass (as in the case of the margarita); I suggest you try both!

Serves 1

    Ice cubes
2 limes, plus 1 additional lime wedge, for garnish
1 bottle light to medium Mexican beer, preferably Pacífico
    (Bohemia makes a great *michelada* as well)

Fill a chilled glass or beer mug with ice. Cut the limes in half, and squeeze the juice over the cubes. Add the beer, garnish with lime wedge, and enjoy immediately.

from left: Peruvian Peppered Cheese Sauce, Yuca Fries (page 84), and Mexican Beer Cooler

yuca Fries
WITH Peruvian Peppered Cheese sauce

If you mention huancaína *sauce to a Peruvian in the States, you may see*
some tears of nostalgia; this much-beloved salsa is certainly a Peruvian comfort
food. Usually served with boiled potatoes, here it's presented as a dip with very
tasty yuca fries (which are a new favorite of my kids—and many of the kids in our
neighborhood). I've also served this creamy, smooth, and slightly spicy sauce
with roasted potatoes and French fries.

See photo on page 83
Makes about 25 fries and 1 cup of sauce

Sauce

2	tablespoons plus ¼ cup canola oil
1	medium sweet yellow onion, minced
1	garlic clove, crushed
3	hard-cooked egg yolks
8	ounces Mexican white cheese (or ricotta or feta cheese)
1½	tablespoons *ají amarillo* (sold in large supermarkets and Latin markets), or to taste
¼	teaspoon achiote (ground annatto seeds, sold in large supermarkets and Latin markets; optional)
¼	cup evaporated milk
3	saltine crackers
1	lemon, cut in half
	Freshly ground black pepper

Yuca Fries

    One 24-ounce bag frozen yuca

    Chicken broth or salted water

    Vegetable oil for frying

    Kosher salt

Prepare the sauce: Heat the 2 tablespoons of oil over medium heat in a frying pan and sauté the onion and garlic, stirring constantly, for about 5 minutes, or until the onion has softened.

In a food processor, combine the egg yolks, cheese, *ají*, achiote, milk, and crackers. Add the onion mixture and process until well blended. Gradually pour in the ¼ cup of oil and mix until creamy. The sauce will be a pale yellow color. Squeeze the lemon halves and stir in the juice. Add black pepper to taste. Serve immediately, or cover and refrigerate for up to two days. Return to room temperature before serving.

Then prepare the yuca fries: Cook the frozen yuca in a stockpot of chicken broth or salted water. Bring to a boil and cook for about 20 minutes, or until tender. Be careful: You don't want to overcook the yuca or it will get mushy. Drain and let cool. Cut the yuca in half, and remove the stringy core. Then cut into pieces about ½ inch thick and 2 inches long.

Heat about 1½ inches of oil in a heavy pot. Fry the yuca, in small batches, for 5 to 7 minutes, or until golden. Drain on paper towels. Toss with salt, transfer to a platter, and serve immediately with the sauce.

Guacamole with Grapes & Nuts

It's hard to resist the nutty flavor of avocado flesh; it can be eaten with just a squirt of lemon or lime and a sprinkle of salt, used as a topping for soups and salads, or served as a backdrop in various guacamoles and salsas. This interpretation of guacamole—with a bit of spark and smoke from chipotles, *sweet from the grapes, and crunch from the nuts—is a crowd pleaser! Serve this with a bowl of tortilla chips and Pineapple Champagne Cocktail (page 15) or Sangría Blanca (page 94).*

Makes about 2 cups

2	ripe Hass avocados, peeled, pitted, and coarsely chopped
¼	red onion, finely diced
	Juice of 1 lime
½	teaspoon *chipotle* purée (purée 1 small can of *chipotle en adobo*)
15 to 20	seedless red grapes, halved
⅓	cup toasted walnuts, coarsely chopped and toasted
	Kosher salt and freshly ground black pepper to taste
¼	cup chopped fresh cilantro

In a large bowl, combine the avocado, red onion, and lime juice. Stir in the *chipotle* purée and grapes, but don't mix too much or the avocado will get mushy. At this point, you may want to refrigerate the guacamole (with the avocado pit, so the browning is lessened). Just before serving, remove the pit. Add the toasted walnuts and salt and pepper, and stir. Sprinkle the cilantro on top and serve.

Fruit is festive! Most of these drinks are fun not only because they're colorful and tasty, but also because you can do a lot of the prep work ahead of time and spend more time with your guests.

sangrías, punches & fruit-filled cocktails

Chilean Strawberry Pisco Punch

CHILEAN STRAWBERRY PISCO PUNCH

Both Chile and Peru claim pisco as their own. As a result, both countries boast a large selection of cocktails and punches made from their much-beloved brandy. Though the flavor of pisco may vary slightly depending on the particular grape used to create it, its delicate taste combines beautifully with a variety of fruit flavors. This simple strawberry punch has spark! Just as with sangría, you can use either white or red wine. Serve on a steamy summer evening with Empanaditas de Carne (page 12) or any of your favorite tapas.

Serves 4 to 6

- 1 cup strawberries, stemmed and sliced
- ½ cup superfine sugar, or to taste
- ¾ cup pisco
- 1 bottle dry white or red wine, chilled
- 2 cups ice cubes

Combine the strawberries with the sugar and pisco. Cover and refrigerate for half an hour. Pour the wine into a pitcher filled with ice. Pour the pisco mixture on top, stir, and serve immediately.

brazilian mango-coconut punch

Brazil's cocktails—like its cuisine—contain many African elements. Ingredients such as coconut milk, also found in the Caribbean regions of Latin America, are not uncommon. This smooth milky-white punch, which combines fresh fruit and coconut milk with lime and cachaça, *Brazil's national alcohol, goes down so easily, you may be tempted to drink it quickly! Though this punch marries quite well with Brazilian Cheese Puffs (page 30), it can be served with just about any appetizer.*

Serves 4

   One 14-ounce can coconut milk
1 fresh mango, peeled, cut from pit, and finely diced, or ¾ cup mango nectar
   Juice of 2 limes plus 4 half-moon lime slices, for garnish
2 cups ice cubes
¼ cup granulated sugar, or to taste
6 ounces *cachaça* or white rum

In a blender, combine the coconut milk, mango, lime juice, and ice. Add the sugar and cachaça and process until well blended. Pour into chilled wine or cocktail glasses, garnish with the lime slices, and serve immediately.

tropical fruit punch

Any visit to the Caribbean will introduce you to a wealth of rum cocktails.
These drinks help conjure up a luscious image of sipping while sitting under a
swaying palm tree. Well, this is one of those prepare-in-a-blender-while-
you're-out-at-poolside drinks! And for those who don't drink alcohol, the
nonalcoholic version is just as tasty.

Serves about 8

- 2 cups mango nectar
- 2 cups guava nectar
- 1 cup unsweetened pineapple juice
- ½ cup cream of coconut, or to taste, well mixed
  Juice of 1 lime
- 12 ounces amber (gold) rum
  Ice cubes
  Fresh pineapple wedges, for garnish

Combine the mango nectar, guava nectar, pineapple juice, cream of coconut,
and lime juice in a large pitcher. At this point, you can cover and refrigerate the
punch for up to 1 day. Before using, mix well and stir in the rum. Combine
1 cup of punch and 1 cup of ice cubes in a blender and blend until smooth and
thick. Pour into glasses. Garnish with fresh pineapple wedges and serve.

RED WINE SANGRÍA WITH PINEAPPLE

One of the best sangrías I had was on the island of Menorca, off the coast of Spain. Sitting at a table in a gorgeous open-air café, listening to the waves crash against the rocks not too far from us and watching the sunset, a friend and I enjoyed sangría served from a beautiful ceramic pitcher. I remember the waiter using a wooden spoon to hold back the fruit as he poured the drink, and then using that same spoon to divide the wine-soaked fruit into our glasses. Sangría is the ultimate party punch: It's romantic, delicious, easy to adapt—and you can prepare it hours before serving. In Spain every restaurant has its own recipe, which is typically a mix of wine, brandy, and fresh fruits, served over ice. Numerous variations can be found throughout the Americas, and you should certainly experiment with your own favorite wine-and-fruit combinations. This sangría is perfect for a fall luncheon (or cocktail party), served with Toasted Butternut Squash Salad (page 102) and Tortilla Española (page 72).

Serves 2 to 4

- ½ ripe pineapple, peeled and cut into ¼-inch chunks
     Juice of 3 lemons, plus 4 half-moon lemon slices, for garnish
- 3   tablespoons superfine sugar, or to taste
- 1   bottle red Rioja, or any medium-bodied dry red wine you enjoy
     Ice cubes

Combine the pineapple chunks, lemon juice, and sugar. Stir and combine with the red wine. Refrigerate for at least 4 hours or overnight. Prior to serving, add plenty of ice and garnish with the lemon slices. Serve in wine glasses. Be sure to add some of the wine-soaked pineapple to each glass.

passion fruit sangría

Intense, fragrant, and mysteriously tropical, passion fruit's unique flavor is inspiring.
This sangría is a marvelous summertime party punch. Though the fresh passion
fruit may not be easy to come by in most areas of the United States, unsweetened frozen
passion fruit purée, as well as concentrated forms, can be found in most Latin
American groceries. (If you find passion fruit nectar, you won't need the sugar.)
Prepare your sangría in the morning, so that the flavors have time to blend, and you
can relax and enjoy the party with your guests! Make sure you serve this one in a
glass pitcher so that your guests can admire the gorgeous colors of the sunset-orange
passion fruit and the slim flashes of light green from the apples and lime slices.

Serves 4 to 6

1 cup fresh-squeezed orange juice

1 cup passion fruit purée,
   frozen and thawed, diluted
   passion fruit concentrate,
   or passion fruit nectar

   Juice of 2 limes,
   plus 6 half-moon lime slices

¼ cup mango nectar

2 tablespoons superfine sugar,
   or to taste (use more if your
   passion fruit is unsweetened)

3 tablespoons Cointreau

1 bottle dry white wine

6 half-moon orange slices

2 Granny Smith apples, cored and
   cut into eighths

In a large pitcher, combine the juices, nectar, sugar, Cointreau, and white wine.
Stir in the lime, orange, and apple slices. Cover and refrigerate for at least 2 hours, or
overnight. Stir well and pour into wine glasses. Use a spoon to add some fruit
to each glass. Serve.

sangría blanca

*This white and tropical version of the Spanish original is great for parties —
and it looks gorgeous in a glass pitcher with a tall wooden spoon. You can make it a
day ahead of time (to let the flavors blend), and then serve it chilled from the
refrigerator, with appetizers like Walnut- & Cabrales-Coated Grapes (page 96).*

Serves 6 to 8

½   cup superfine sugar, or to taste
¼   cup water
2   bottles dry white wine
½   cup mango nectar
    Juice of 1 orange
    Juice of 1 lime
1   mango, peeled, seeded, and cut into ¼-inch dice
½   cup diced papaya (¼-inch cubes)
½   cup diced pineapple (¼-inch cubes)

In a small saucepan over medium heat, combine the sugar and water and cook,
stirring constantly, until the sugar has dissolved. Remove from the heat and let cool
to room temperature.

Meanwhile, combine the wine, mango nectar, orange and lime juices, mango,
papaya, and pineapple in a pitcher. Stir in the sugar mixture. Cover tightly and
refrigerate for at least 2 hours, or up to 1 day. Taste and adjust sugar as needed
before serving. Pour into glasses; use a spoon to scoop up some fruit into
the glasses. Serve.

Walnut- & Cabrales-Coated Grapes (page 96) and Sangría Blanca

walnut- & cabrales-coated grapes

Though this appetizer is popular in Buenos Aires, Argentina, it was my friend Koen—a Belgian who lives in Mexico—who recently brought this wonderful treat to my attention. Cabrales, a Spanish blue cheese, is deliciously balanced by the sweet meat of the grapes and the blanket of crunchy nuts in this dish. If you can't find Cabrales, Gorgonzola or Roquefort are just fine. Don't be afraid to vary the blue cheese-to-cream cheese ratio, depending on your preference.

See photo on page 95
Serves 10 to 12

1 ¼	cups walnut or pecan halves
6	ounces Cabrales, Gorgonzola, or Roquefort cheese
6	ounces cream cheese, at room temperature
1	pound (between 40 and 50) seedless red grapes
½	teaspoon chopped fresh parsley (optional)

Preheat the oven to 350°F. Spread the nuts out on a sheet pan, and toast them in the oven for 5 to 8 minutes, or until fragrant and lightly toasted. Set aside to cool.

Meanwhile, combine the Cabrales and cream cheese in a food processor and process until pretty smooth (a few small lumps are fine). Coat the clean, dry grapes with the cream-cheese mixture (it's easiest—but messiest—to do this with your hands, without any utensils) by scooping a bit up in your fingers and using your fingers to make sure each one is well covered. They won't be uniformly covered—and that's okay. Place the coated grapes on a plate, lightly cover with plastic wrap, and refrigerate for 15 minutes.

Meanwhile, in a food processor or by hand, chop the toasted nuts and spread them on a platter or baking sheet.

Once the grapes have been lightly chilled, remove them from the fridge and individually roll them in the chopped toasted nuts so that they are well coated. Cover again, and refrigerate until ready to serve. You can even prepare the grapes a day before serving. If the grapes are small enough, you can serve them whole. Otherwise, you may want to cut them in half and place them on a serving platter. Insert toothpicks or have them nearby. Sprinkle them with a bit of parsley just before serving, if desired.

papaya, pineapple & banana rum punch

Smooth and soothing, this rum punch is simply delightful.

Serves 4

- ½ ripe papaya, peeled, seeded, and diced
- ½ pineapple, peeled and diced
- 1 banana, peeled and sliced
- 6 ounces light or golden rum
- 4 cups fresh orange juice
- 4 cups ice cubes
- Pineapple slices, for garnish

Combine all of the ingredients (except for the pineapple slices for garnish) in a blender, and process until smooth. Garnish with pineapple slices and serve immediately.

summertime-fruit caipiroska

This cocktail is a fun fiesta drink that could almost be served as an appetizer—or even a dessert! This vodka version of the Brazilian classic caipirinha is almost sangría-like in the amount of fruit it contains. And, as in the case of sangría, it offers you a lot of flexibility. You can vary the fruits and the vodka, depending on your and your guests' tastes. It's hard to serve the Summertime-Fruit Caipiroska with a straw because the fruit gets caught in it, but you might want to consider serving it with a spoon!

Serves 4

16 2-inch chunks seedless (or pitted) watermelon

8 strawberries, stemmed and sliced, plus 4 more for garnish

½ fresh pineapple, plus extra pieces for garnish, peeled, cored, and cut into cubes

6 to 8 ounces vodka (1 ½ to 2 ounces per serving)

About 2 cups ice cubes

Divide the fruit into four tumblers. Using a pestle or the end of a wooden spoon, crush the fruit pieces until they're slightly muddled. Divide the vodka and ice cubes among the glasses. Stir to mix. Serve immediately.

Sakerinha

sakerinha

Japanese immigrants to Brazil have had a great culinary influence; even in churrascarías—typical Brazilian restaurants that feature grilled meats—sushi bars are common. The sakerinha, which is a caipirinha made with sake, is an example of the fusion of the Brazilian and Japanese cultures. This version, almost an appetizer itself (don't skip eating the sake-soaked strawberries!) complements any dish it's served with.

Serves 1

- 4   strawberries, stemmed and sliced, plus 1 strawberry for garnish
- 1   teaspoon superfine sugar, or to taste
- 2   ounces sake
    Ice cubes

Place the strawberries and sugar in a tall bar glass. Use a pestle or the end of a wooden spoon to mash the strawberries and sugar together. Add the sake and stir. Add ice, cover, and shake. Pour into a glass, garnish with the strawberry, and serve immediately.

Toasted Butternut Squash Salad

Squash is found in many dishes throughout the Americas. Here the sweet toasted butternut squash offers a nice backdrop to the smooth nutty flavor of the Gruyère cheese and the crunchy, salty taste of the peanuts. This fabulous autumnal salad, ideally served on small plates that your guests can pick up as they enjoy their cocktails, can be made with or without the meat.

Makes 6 to 8 portions

2 cups fresh, peeled, and cubed (½-inch pieces) butternut squash

3 tablespoons olive oil

1 teaspoon unsalted butter

1 tablespoon dark brown sugar

  Kosher salt and freshly ground pepper

2 teaspoons balsamic vinegar

  Leaves from 1 sprig fresh thyme

½ cup salted peanuts

1 bunch red leaf lettuce, washed and ripped into bite-size pieces

1 bunch romaine lettuce, washed and cut into bite-size pieces

8 ounces Gruyère cheese, cut into thin ¼-inch-wide strips

8 ounces *jamón serrano* or *prosciutto di Parma*,
    cut into thin ¼-inch-wide strips (optional)

In a medium-size pot filled with slightly salted water, cook the squash for about 10 to 12 minutes or until tender. Drain well.

In a frying pan, heat 1 tablespoon of the oil and the teaspoon of butter. Add the drained squash. Add the sugar, salt, and pepper, and cook over medium heat, letting the squash caramelize, for 5 to 7 minutes. Add the balsamic vinegar and thyme leaves and cook until the liquid evaporates. Remove from the heat.

In a smaller frying pan, heat 1 tablespoon of oil and toast the peanuts until golden, about 3 minutes.

Take out a quarter of the squash, and place it in a food processor or blender. Slowly add about a tablespoon of olive oil (or more) until the dressing reaches the thickness you would like.

Combine the lettuces in a large wooden bowl. Toss with the squash dressing, cheese, and prosciutto. Top with the toasted peanuts and serve.

Frozen papaya-Rum cocktail

You can double or triple this recipe, freeze it for a while, and then bring it out to serve with your warm treats!

Serves 2

- 3 ounces light rum
- 1 ounce coconut rum
  Juice of ½ lime
- ¾ cup chopped ripe papaya
- 1 teaspoon superfine sugar, or to taste
- 1 cup ice cubes
- 2 slices star fruit, for garnish

Combine all of the ingredients except the ice cubes and star fruit in a blender and process until smooth. Add the ice cubes and blend again. Pour into chilled margarita or cocktail glasses and garnish with the star fruit. Serve immediately.

Frozen Papaya-Rum Cocktail

Arepas

Commonly found in both Venezuela and Colombia (and now in Latin markets across the United States), these corncakes, with their fine flavor, ease of preparation, and flexibility, are sure to win you over! Arepas are one of those treats that once you learn to make, you'll want to incorporate immediately into your repertoire and vary according to your liking. They can be served alone, with salsas, or in Panuchos (page 48) and are easy to reheat in the microwave or toaster. You can try adding fresh corn, peppers, mushrooms, and different cheeses for variety. Here I've added my kids' favorite cheese—mozzarella—and a bit of sugar to the traditional recipe.

Makes 40 small *arepas*

1 ½ cups instant white (or yellow) cornmeal (*harina precocida* in Spanish)

2   cups hot water (can be from the tap)

½   cup grated mozzarella

¼   cup sugar

½   teaspoon kosher salt

Butter or oil for frying

Pour the cornmeal into a large bowl and while mixing with a wooden spoon, gradually pour in the hot water. Add the mozzarella, sugar, and salt and mix, using your hands, until there are no lumps. Cover and let sit for 5 minutes, or you can refrigerate the dough and keep it for up to a day. When you're ready to make the *arepas*, scoop up a heaping teaspoon of dough and form a small pancake (about 1 ½ inches wide) in the palm of your hand. Repeat with the remaining dough, and set aside on a platter.

Lightly butter or oil a griddle or heavy skillet. Cook the *arepas* for about 3 to 4 minutes on each side, or until golden. (You may need to wipe out the frying pan with a paper towel after a few batches so that the butter doesn't blacken.) Serve immediately.

Just as a romantic goodbye kiss may leave you smiling, so will these drinks! These coffee and dessert drinks can be a lovely finish…or perhaps, in some cases, a beginning.

coffee & dessert drinks

Brazilian Coffee Cocktail

Brazilian Coffee Cocktail

This tasty—and powerful—dessert drink is similar to a White Russian.

Serves 1

1 ½   ounces *cachaça* (Brazilian rum)
1   ounce Kahlúa
   Ice cubes
1   tablespoon heavy cream

Pour the *cachaça* and Kahlúa into a short chilled glass (or wine glass)
with ice. Float the cream on top by pouring it over the round side of a spoon.
Serve immediately.

café de cuba

Cuban coffee is always wonderful; this dessert coffee is a great way to finish a cocktail party!

Serves 1

1 ½	ounces dark rum
¾	ounce crème de cacao, plus more to drizzle on top
4	ounces hot, strong coffee
2 to 3	tablespoons sweetened whipped heavy cream

Pour the rum and crème de cacao into a coffee glass. Add the hot coffee. Top with the whipped cream and a drizzle of crème de cacao. Serve immediately.

café mexicano

Quite festive—and often flaming—Mexican coffees vary depending on the region and, of course, the host (or restaurant). Coffee, chocolate, and cinnamon are flavors that are often found together in Mexico; you may want to vary the amounts of each depending on your own likes.

Serves 1

1	teaspoon turbinado or coarse brown sugar
4	ounces hot coffee
2	ounces Kahlúa or Tía María, plus more to drizzle on top
2 to 3	tablespoons whipped sweetened heavy cream
	Dash ground cinnamon
¼	teaspoon grated semisweet chocolate
1	cinnamon stick, for garnish

Moisten the rim of a coffee glass using your fingertip and water. Spread the sugar on a saucer, and press the rim of the glass into it, turning gently until the rim is evenly coated. Pour in the hot coffee and Kahlúa. Add the whipped cream to the center (so that you don't ruin your sugar rim). Sprinkle on the cinnamon and chocolate. Top with a drizzle of liqueur, if desired, add the cinnamon stick, and serve.

peruvian winter wine

Though Limeñan winters can hardly be compared to, say, New York winters, it does get cloudy, damp, and chilly there. This warm wine drink is perfect for those days.

Serves about 8

1 ½ cups water
 ¾ cup granulated sugar, or according to taste
    Rind from 1 medium-size orange
    Rind from 1 lemon, plus additional rinds, for garnish
  4 cinnamon sticks, plus additional sticks for garnish
 12 cloves
  3 cups red wine (preferably a Chilean Cabernet)

Fill a medium-size saucepan with the water, sugar, and orange and lemon rinds and bring to a boil. Add the four cinnamon sticks and the cloves. Lower the heat and simmer for 20 minutes. Strain into a thermos or heatproof pitcher. Add the wine and serve immediately in wine glasses garnished with additional lemon rinds and cinnamon sticks.

Peruvian Winter Wine

cola de mono

The history of this Chilean cocktail, which is a chilled coffee traditionally served during their warm Christmas and New Year's holidays, is one that varies depending on whom you consult. The recipe also has several variations; some use a vanilla bean instead of cinnamon, others add cloves. Literally translated as "monkey tail," the name may refer to the bottles it was originally kept in, Anís de Mono, *which feature a monkey with a very long tail. Others say the name refers to a former Chilean president, Pedro Montt, and that it was originally named Colt de Montt, after his revolver!* Cola de Mono, *served straight up, should be made ahead and chilled in the refrigerator prior to serving. Try serving it as an after-brunch drink on a steamy summer day!*

Serves 4

- 2　cups milk
- 3　tablespoons superfine sugar, or to taste
- 1　tablespoon espresso coffee, either prepared or instant
　　Pinch nutmeg, plus extra for garnish
- 1　cinnamon stick
- 2　ounces pisco, or to taste

In a medium-size saucepan, heat the milk, sugar, coffee, nutmeg, and cinnamon stick just to a boil, stirring frequently. As soon as the sugar dissolves, remove the pan from the heat and chill to room temperature. Once cooled, remove the cinnamon stick and stir in the pisco. Cover and chill in the refrigerator. Sprinkle a dash of nutmeg on top of each glass just prior to serving.

acknowledgments

Muchísimas gracias to my terrific agent Jane Dystel, as well as Stacey Glick and Miriam Goderich at Dystel & Goderich Literary Management, for all their help and support; my fabulously enthusiastic editor, Jennifer Lang and the rest of the team at STC; the wonderfully creative designer, Lana Lê; the incredibly talented photographer, Dasha Wright; and the fantastic food stylist, Brett Kurzweil. *Gracias* to my friends around the globe—especially Maria Rosa in Argentina, Elizabeth in Brazil, Wady in Costa Rica, Christian in Chile, Koen and Alex in Mexico, Cynthia and Marita from Peru, Hugo from Colombia, and many, many more who offered their palates, comments, and suggestions. Thanks also to my wonderful family and friends: my parents, Sonia and Tony Gargagliano; Amy Magee, my sister-in-law; Ronna Corlin, Karen Johnson, Lisa Spielvogel, and Alexander Smalls; my Glenwood Lake neighbors: Michael and Monica; Michael and Amelia, who at a moment's notice would rush over to sample cocktails and tapas; and the ESL students, teachers, and staff of the New Rochelle and White Plains Public Libraries, all of whom inspire me on a daily basis.

conversion charts

The weights and measurements given below are not exact equivalents but have been rounded up or down slightly to make measuring easier.

weight equivalents

AVOIRDUPOIS	METRIC
¼ oz	7 g
½ oz	15 g
1 oz	30 g
2 oz	60 g
3 oz	90 g
4 oz	115 g
5 oz	150 g
6 oz	175 g
7 oz	200 g
8 oz (½ lb)	25 g
9 oz	250 g
10 oz	300 g
11 oz	325 g
12 oz	350 g
13 oz	375 g
14 oz	400 g
15 oz	425 g
16 oz (1 lb)	450 g
1½ lb	750 g
2 lb	900 g
2¼ lb	1.0 kg
3 lb	1.4 kg
4 lb	1.8 kg

volume equivalents

AMERICAN	METRIC	IMPERIAL
¼ t	1.2 ml	
½ t	2.5 ml	
1 t	5.0 ml	
½ T (1.5 t)	7.5 ml	
1 T (3 t)	15 ml	
¼ cup (4 T)	60 ml	2 fl oz
⅓ cup (5 T)	75 ml	2½ fl oz
½ cup (8 T)	125 ml	4 fl oz
⅔ cup (10 T)	150 ml	5 fl oz
¾ cup (12 T)	175 ml	6 fl oz
1 cup (16 T)	250 ml	8 fl oz
1¼ cups	300 ml	10 fl oz (½ pt)
1½ cups	350 ml	12 fl oz
2 cups (1 pint)	500 ml	16 fl oz
2½ cups	625 ml	20 fl oz (1 pint)
1 quart	1 liter	32 fl oz

oven temperature equivalents

OVEN MARK	F	C	GAS
Very cool	250–275	130–140	½ – 1
Cool	300	150	2
Warm	325	170	3
Moderate	350	180	4
Moderately hot	375	190	5
	400	200	6
Hot	425	220	7
	450	230	8
Very hot	475	250	9

index